OUR AMAZING CONTINENTS

Continents are the largest pieces of land
on Earth. There are seven continents.
The largest is Asia. The other continents,
from largest to smallest, are Africa,
North America, South America, Antarctica,
Europe, and Australia. Each continent's
landscape has shaped the lives of its
animals, plants, and people.

Library of Congress Cataloging-in-Publication Data
Sayre, April Pulley.
Greetings, Asia! / April Pulley Sayre.
        p. cm. — (Our amazing continents)
Summary: Introduces the continent of Asia, looking at its geography,
plant and animal life, weather, and settlement by humans.
ISBN 0-7613-2124-1 (lib. bdg.)   ISBN 0-7613-1991-3 (pbk.)
1. Asia—Geography—Juvenile literature. 2. Natural
history—Asia—Juvenile literature. [1. Asia.] I. Title.
DS5.92 .S29 2003   915—dc21   2002151204

Cover photographs courtesy of Sovfoto/Eastfoto (front cover) and
TASS/Sovfoto (back cover)

Photographs courtesy of NASA: p. 1; Photo Researchers, Inc.: pp. 3
(© Bryan & Cherry Alexander), 4 (© Alain Thomas/Explorer), 5 (top right: ©
Tim Davis; bottom: © Carleton Ray), 8-9 (© Carl Purcell), 14 (© Bryan &
Cherry Alexander), 15 (top: Gary Meszaros), 22 (© George Gerster), 24
(© Art Wolfe), 25 (bottom: © Tom McHugh), 26 (top: © E. Hanumantha
Rao; bottom: © Paul Stepan), 27 (© Gregory Ochocki), 29 (bottom:
© Leroux PH/Explorer), 30 (© George Chan); National Geographic Society
Image Collection: pp. 5 (top left: © Michael K. Nichols), 13 (top: © Sarah
Leen), 16 (© Maria Stenzel), 21 (© Richard T. Nowitz), 23 (© Paul Chesley);
Photri, Inc.: p 6; Visuals Unlimited, Inc.: pp. 9 (© Joe McDonald), 15
(bottom: © Hugh Rose), 17 (© William J. Weber); Tom Stack & Associates:
pp. 10 (© Spencer Swanger), 11 (top left: © Erwin & Peggy Bauer), 28
(bottom: © Novastock); Peter Arnold, Inc.: pp. 11 (top right: © Ed Reschke),
12-13 (© Peter Arnold), 25 (top: © Roland Seitre); Woodfin Camp &
Associates: pp. 11 (bottom: © Mike Yamashita), 18 (© Mike Yamashita), 19
(© T. Stoddart/Katz), 28 (top: © Catherine Karnow), 29 (top: © Robert
Frerck); Corbis: pp. 13 (bottom: © Richard T. Nowitz); Sovfoto/Eastfoto:
p. 20 (© R. I'Anson); Bruce Coleman, Inc. (© Hans Reinhard): p. 31. Map
on p. 32 by Joe LeMonnier

Published by The Millbrook Press, Inc.
2 Old New Milford Road
Brookfield, Connecticut 06804

Reindeer herd in Siberia

GREETINGS,
ASIA!

APRIL PULLEY SAYRE

THE MILLBROOK PRESS, BROOKFIELD, CONNECTICUT

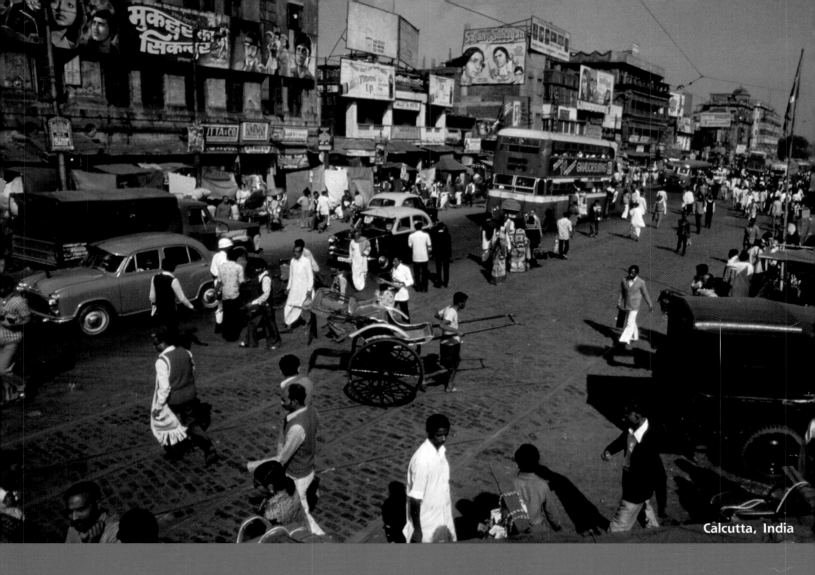

Calcutta, India

Have you met Asia?
It's Earth's largest continent.

A Komodo dragon, largest of the monitor lizards

Giant panda

It's a land of busy cities and many cultures. It has tall mountains, tremendous deserts, coral reefs, and rain forests. It's home to pandas, monitor lizards, and walruses.

Walruses

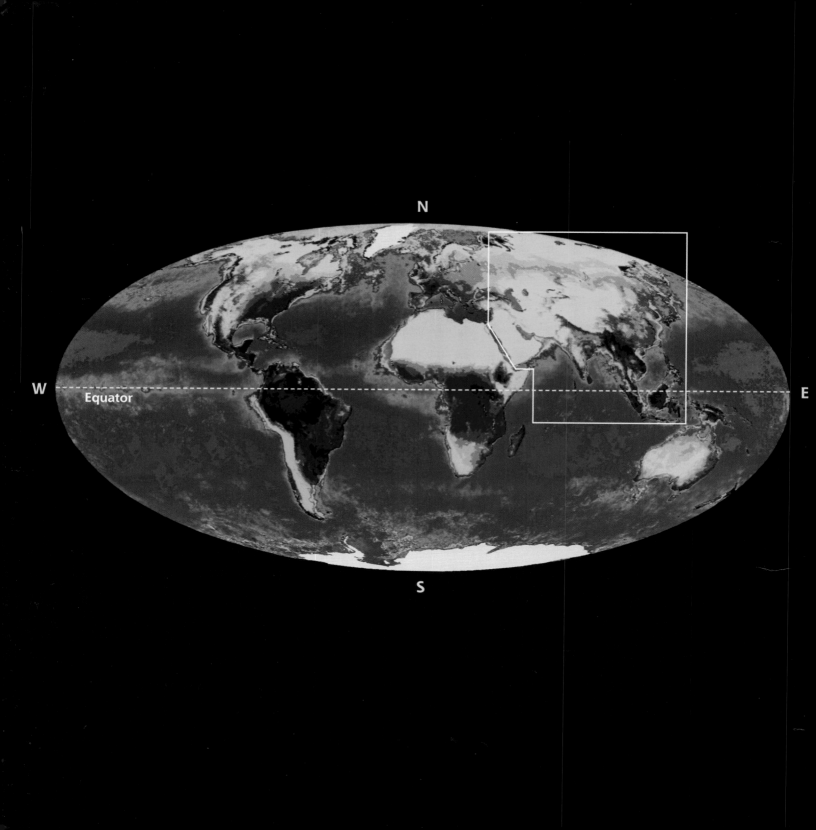

Asia stretches far and wide. It is bigger than North and South America, combined.

Asia and Europe share one big piece of land. Some geographers call this large piece of land Eurasia. They consider Eurasia to be one continent. Others say Asian and European history and culture are so different that Asia and Europe should be considered separate continents. These geographers divide the landmass at the Ural Mountain range. Six countries are partly in Asia, partly in Europe: Russia, Turkey, Kazakhstan, Georgia, Armenia, and Azerbaijan.

Dunes of the Gobi desert in China

White-backed vulture

Asia has many deserts.

In Asia's deserts, wild cats hunt and gerbils hop. In some areas, deserts are pebbly. Other desert areas have mounds of sand called dunes. Vultures soar above the hot desert sand. Snakes hide out in the shade until night falls and the desert cools.

Desert plants are scarce. Wildflowers sprout after rain. But in a desert it may not rain for months or years!

A cloud-covered Mount Everest

Asia contains Earth's highest mountains, the Himalayas.

Asia's Mount Everest is Earth's highest peak. It towers 29,035 feet (8,850 meters) high. Asia has other high places called plateaus. Plateaus are high, but flatter on top than mountains.

Snow leopards, ibex, and yaks live in Asia's mountains.

Some mountain people in Central Asia herd shaggy cattle called yaks. Yaks provide milk, meat, a way to carry loads, and hair to make yarn for clothing. Yak droppings, when dry, are burned for heat.

Snow leopard

Ibex

Yak on the Tibetan plateau

Asia has tremendous lakes.

Baikal seals

Israeli resort on Red Sea

Lake Baikal

Russia's Lake Baikal is Earth's oldest, deepest lake. Baikal is more than a mile deep. Baikal seals are one of over a thousand animal species that are found only in the lake.

Even though they are called "seas," the Aral Sea, Caspian Sea, and Dead Sea are lakes because they are completely surrounded by land. The Aral Sea is very salty. The Caspian Sea is Earth's largest lake. The Dead Sea is Earth's lowest place on land. Its shoreline is below sea level.

In the summer shallow pools may form on the tundra, but the land underneath stays frozen.

The tundra is treeless, lumpy land, with low-growing plants.

It has cold, icy places. Northern Asia is cold and snowy in winter. But in summer, walruses, reindeer, arctic terns, Siberian cranes, and bean geese raise their young on the tundra.

Arctic tern

South of the tundra is the taiga, a kind of forest.

Most taiga trees have cones and narrow leaves called needles.

Moose, red squirrels, and great grey owls live in Russia's taiga.

A bull moose forages on the taiga.

Not many people live in the highest, driest, or coldest parts of Asia.

A caravan of traders in Tibet. It will take 5 days to reach the next village.

Bactrian camels

The Gobi Desert, in China, is mostly uninhabited. The Gobi is hot in summer but very cold in winter.

Bactrian camels, which have two humps, live in the Gobi.

A camel's hump is not filled with water. It's made of fat. But as the camel's body uses up this fat, the fat provides water within its body.

Mekong River junction, Vietnam

Most of Asia's people live in warm, wetter places along rivers and coastlines.

Ganges River

Rivers are important in people's lives. Rivers provide drinking water, fish, water for crops, and a place to wash clothes.

People live in boats along the Mekong River, which flows through China, Myanmar, Laos, Thailand, Cambodia, and Vietnam.

The Ganges River, in India, is considered sacred. It is a place for special ceremonies.

Rains and floods shape people's lives.

Some Asian countries have many months without rain. The weather gets hotter and drier. Then, suddenly, the monsoon rains begin. People welcome the monsoon rains even though the heavy rains flood streets. The rains mean the weather will soon turn cooler. Fish, frogs, birds, and crocodiles raise their families in and along ponds and rivers filled by the rains.

Monsoon season, India

Water buffalo in a flooded field

Heavy rains can cause rivers to spill out of their channels. China's Huang river sometimes floods, sweeping away roads and buildings. Bangladesh, which is a low-lying country, has many floods, too. Floods can be dangerous to people. But flooding rivers do have a good side. Rivers carry rich soil onto nearby farmlands.

After the floodwaters go down, the soil is better for farming.

Krakatau, an active volcano island

Morning glory vines grow in volcanic ash on Krakatau.

Eastern and southeastern Asia have many volcanoes.

Many of Indonesia's 17,000 islands are volcanoes. In 1883 the Indonesian island of Krakatau exploded as it erupted. Two-thirds of the island was destroyed. After the eruption, the land seemed lifeless. But since then, plant seeds have floated on wind and water to the island. Animals have come to the island, too. A forest is now growing on Krakatau.

Some of Asia's southern islands have rain forests.

Rain forests are warm and rainy, with very tall trees. During some years large numbers of trees bloom all at once. Petals flutter down, covering the forest floor with bright colors.

Orangutan in Borneo rainforest

Two Filipino kids help the photographer by holding a flying fox's large wings

Asia's rain forests are full of amazing animals.

Orangutans, gibbons, hornbills, and birds of paradise live in Asia's rain forests. Flying geckos glide from tree to tree. Flapping through the forests are flying foxes, which are the world's biggest bats, with a wingspan 5 feet (1.7 meters) wide.

Flying gecko

Mangrove swamps and coral reefs grow near Asia's southern shores.

Tigers

Mangroves are trees that can grow with their roots in water. Mudskippers, storks, herons, crocodiles, and tigers inhabit India's mangrove swamps. Mangroves are important nurseries for fish and birds.

Mangrove forest

Nearby are underwater ridges made by tiny animals: corals.

The ridges are coral reefs. Colorful fish swim among the corals. Coral reefs grow near the Indonesian islands. There are also coral reefs in the Red Sea.

Part of a coral reef in Thailand

Vietnam

Asia has more people than any other continent.

More than half the people on Earth live in Asia. Asia has many large cities such as Tokyo, Bombay, Manila, Bangkok, Tel Aviv, Calcutta, and Moscow.

China

Kids in Turkey jumping rope

The streets are filled with cars, bikes, and people. People of many cultures and languages live together in cities. The people of Asia have a wonderful variety of foods, clothes, arts, crafts, religions, beliefs, and customs.

Boys from the country of Sri Lanka

Just when you think you know Asia, something else about it surprises you.

Maybe it's wild tulips in the mountains, or the spiraling horns of argali sheep. Maybe it's the sound of a song, or a floating food market, or somebody's smile. It seems you're always just getting to know Asia. Greetings, Asia, the largest continent on Earth!

How do you get to know the face of a continent?

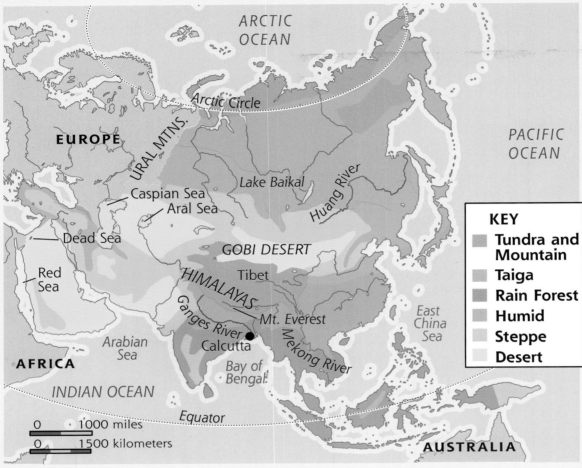

ASIA

ARCTIC OCEAN

Arctic Circle

URAL MTNS.

EUROPE

PACIFIC OCEAN

Caspian Sea
Aral Sea

Lake Baikal

Huang River

Dead Sea

GOBI DESERT

Red Sea

HIMALAYAS

Tibet

Ganges River

Mt. Everest

East China Sea

Arabian Sea

Calcutta

Mekong River

AFRICA

Bay of Bengal

INDIAN OCEAN

Equator

0   1000 miles

0   1500 kilometers

AUSTRALIA

KEY
- Tundra and Mountain
- Taiga
- Rain Forest
- Humid
- Steppe
- Desert

Books are one way. This book is about the natural features of a continent. Maps are another way. You can discover the heights of mountains and the depths of valleys by looking at a topographical map. A political map will show you the outlines of countries and locations of cities and towns.

Globes are a third way to learn about the land you live on. Because globes are Earth-shaped, they show more accurately how big the continents are, and where they are. Maps show an Earth that is squashed flat, so the positions and sizes of continents are slightly distorted. A globe can help you imagine what an astronaut sees when looking at our planet from space. Perhaps one day you'll fly into space and see it for yourself! Then you can gaze down at the brown faces of continents, and the blue of the oceans, and the white clouds floating around Earth.